Congress off the Record

ROUNDTABLE PARTICIPANTS

Seven Members of the Class of 1978
United States House of Representatives

William J. Baroody, Jr.
President
American Enterprise Institute

Congress Project Staff Members
American Enterprise Institute
John F. Bibby
Michael J. Malbin
Thomas E. Mann
Norman J. Ornstein

Congress off the Record

The Candid Analyses of Seven Members

Edited by John F. Bibby

 American Enterprise Institute for Public Policy Research
Washington and London

John F. Bibby is professor of political science at the University of Wisconsin-Milwaukee, an adjunct scholar at the American Enterprise Institute, and codirector of AEI's Congress Project.

Library of Congress Cataloging in Publication Data
Main entry under title:

Congress off the record.

    (AEI studies ; 383)
    "Roundtable participants: seven members of the Class
of 1978 United States House of Representatives;
William J. Baroody, Jr., president, American Enterprise
Institute; Congress Project staff members, American
Enterprise Institute, Michael J. Malbin, Thomas E. Mann,
Norman J. Ornstein."
    1. United States. Congress. House. I. Bibby,
John F. II. American Enterprise Institute for Public
Policy Research. III. Series.
JK1319.C63 1983   328.73'072   83-8801
ISBN 0-8447-3526-4

AEI Studies 383

Printed in the United States of America

Contents

1
Introduction

The Congress Project of the American Enterprise Institute was initiated in 1979 to conduct sustained studies of the Congress as an institution. The Congress had undergone immense change in the decade of the 1970s—in its formal rules, informal norms, party structure, staff, and internal distribution of power, and in the recruitment and composition of its membership. We are monitoring the effect of these changes because of their implications for the functioning of representative government and the direction of American public policy.

Freshman members of the Congress, confronting the traditions, leaders, and norms of Congress for the first time, gain a unique view of the House as an institution. We sought to participate in their learning experience as they moved from the status of freshmen to established members of the House leadership structure. Seven members of the class of 1978—that is, representatives elected for the first time in 1978 who began serving their first term in 1979—were invited to participate in a series of roundtable discussions. There they shared with the AEI Congress Project staff their perspectives on life in the House of Representatives.

The seven freshmen participating in the AEI roundtables comprised four Republicans and three Democrats, who represent a variety of ideological viewpoints and diverse constituencies. Their political backgrounds were also diverse. Several had extensive experience in Washington and national politics; others had served in leadership positions in state legislatures and administrations; and some had held no prior elective office, though they had been active in local politics. No claim is made that these members are necessarily representative of the class of 1978. Indeed, we believe that they are an unusually able and aggressive sample of the class. This judgment was confirmed in 1980 when all members of the roundtable group were

1

easily reelected to the Ninety-seventh Congress (1981–1982) and a number of them gained leadership positions within their parties and on committees.

These were post-Watergate members of Congress. By the time of their election in 1978, the furor over Watergate had subsided and the congressional zeal for reform and confrontations with the president had lapsed. These members were not bent on reforming Congress. Rather, they were eager to take advantage of the changes made earlier in the 1970s so that they could participate fully in the legislative process and have an impact on public policy.

We wanted to track the careers of the seven House members at five roundtable discussions held at AEI. These roundtables were conducted evenings after House sessions, between the spring of 1979, during the initial months of the members' first term, through the fall of 1982, at the end of their second term, when they were preparing to face the voters as two-term incumbents. At each session, the participants were assured of anonymity, in order to achieve the most free-wheeling and candid discussions possible. The meetings were tape-recorded and later transcribed.

The roundtable discussions have been reviewed, edited, and arranged by topic in the pages that follow. Because of the pledge of anonymity, the comments are not attributed to specific representatives, and identifying information has been deleted from the quotations.

In analyzing the comments of the members of the House class of 1978, it is essential to keep in mind the political context within which these representatives were functioning. They came to Congress in a midterm election as the president's party suffered the customary electoral setback. Their first term coincided, therefore, with the third and fourth years of the Carter administration—a period when the president's support from the electorate declined, his ability to influence the Congress seriously weakened, and his administration faced a midterm crisis that culminated in the firing of two cabinet officers. During 1978–1979, the Congress and the nation were marking time until the next presidential election. The Ninety-sixth Congress was, therefore, often preoccupied with the politics of the 1980 elections, as members sought to place their parties in the most favorable position for the 1980 elections.

The roundtable group's first election as incumbents was fought against the backdrop of the Reagan-Carter presidential contest, in which several group members played significant campaign roles. Roundtable sessions were held in the spring of 1981, when President Reagan's power and influence with the Congress were at their peak, and in the fall of 1982, just before the midterm elections, when the Democrats sensed a victory and the administration's influence had waned.

The class of 1978 freshmen had, therefore, served under two presidents—one Democrat and one Republican—during periods of presidential ascendency over Congress and of congressional assertiveness. They had confronted a range of controversial issues—budget cuts, tax cuts and tax increases, expanded use of reconciliation in the budget process, increased defense expenditures, the MX missile, nuclear freeze resolutions, the sale of Airborne Warning and Control Systems (AWACS) and other military hardware to the Arabs, financial bailout of the Chrysler Corporation, energy legislation, hospital cost containment, and social security.

Given this range of issues and political circumstances, we believe that the observations of the members of the class of 1978 provide useful and unique insights into the functioning of the House of Representatives in the 1980s. These are insights that only insiders can provide because, unlike the scholars who study Congress, these freshman members lived within the institution on a daily basis. At the same time, because they were new members of a tradition-bound institution, they brought to their observations something of the quality of the critical outsider.

In these discussions, we see evidence of the active role junior members now play in the decision making of the House. Although deference is still paid to those who have acquired expertise through hard work, specialization, and seniority, junior members do not feel an obligation to serve a quiet period of apprenticeship. This is in sharp contrast to the House of the 1950s and 1960s when restrictive norms of behavior prevented junior members from asserting themselves in a constructive manner. These representatives of the class of 1978 show a strong sense of independence—from their party, interest groups, and presidents. In their ambivalence about serving in the House as a career, they stand in sharp contrast to their peers of recent decades who built lifetime careers in House service. The comments of these perceptive members of the class of 1978 convey an image of an institution in transition and, as such, have special value to students of American political institutions.

2
Starting a Career in the House

The nature of a representative's career is usually linked closely to the type of committee assignments he or she receives. It is not surprising, therefore, that new members embark upon committee assignment campaigns almost immediately after winning initial election to the House.

Securing a Committee Assignment

In seeking a committee that will enable one to play a preferred role in the legislative process, freshmen confront the established leadership structure of the House—party leaders, members of the Committee on Committees, state delegation leaders, standing committee members. In the process they learn about the operation of important House work groups and frequently find that they must accommodate their personal preferences to the wishes of more senior and established members.

> Appropriations wasn't what I originally wanted. I wanted Ways and Means and planned to ask for that, and then a senior member from our state said that he wanted to try for it, so I quickly shifted. Luckily that happened early, so it occurred before I sent out letters or anything.
> So I shifted to Appropriations and simply communicated with our Policy and Steering Committee members. During the orientation, I made the rounds to the offices of a good number of those committee members—so that they would put a face with a name—and made my pitch. . . .
> As I visited with the Steering Committee members, several of them would start off with . . . "So what?" "What else is new?" "You want to be on Appropriations." I would tell them that I had been involved in politics for a while and had served as Speaker [in the state legislature] for six years

and that I had had to make some tough decisions. Clearly, that was helpful in the process. . . . I think that in December I saw well over a majority of our Steering and Policy Committee, and in cases where I didn't see them, I saw key staff people. . . .

. . .

In December, I went to see all the Policy and Steering people. And then I wrote letters to those people I didn't get to see. The reason I sought that committee [Public Works and Transportation] was that our city had no representation on it and everybody [in the city delegation] called up, desperate for somebody to be on that committee. So I said, "Okay, why not?"

Then I picked up Post Office and Civil Service as my nonmajor [committee assignment] because in my district we needed a ZIP code change, a very political thing, which I got accomplished. And then the third committee I got was the Select Committee on Aging. Again, that was a political choice. I have 72,000 senior citizens in my district, and I made a campaign promise that I would seek to be on that committee.

. . .

The Women's Caucus asked me if I would go for a spot on Ways and Means. We had lost—when I say "we," I mean the women had lost their sole representative on Ways and Means. But there were two people from my state, who were senior members, who were vying for it, and I was a bit concerned that in [the first two weeks] I was down here, I might antagonize the entire state delegation. So I stayed away from that, and I went for the committees that I did choose.

. . .

I started, I think, like everybody else did, immediately after the election, the morning after as a matter of fact, and called the two top Republicans, Mr. Rhodes and Mr. Michel, whom I already knew.

I asked for Interior, which I got, because it was basically political. It was important to my state, and my Democratic predecessor—the man I replaced—had been chairman of the subcommittee there and a longtime member of the committee.

The second committee was the Ethics Committee, and I took that, really, at the request of the leadership. I was asked if I would serve on that post, and agreed to do so.

. . .

I learned the day after the election that I could forget—

despite my brilliant background as a tax lawyer and whatnot—I could forget Ways and Means, because there was a
gentleman from New Jersey seeking it, and our regional
representative was from New Jersey, and that is the way the
world works, so I rapidly forgot it.

. . .

My bottom line was I had to be on Public Works and I had
to be on the Aviation Subcommittee because I represent the
airport with 25,000 jobs. As the only Republican from my
state, I had little leverage. But the party was very aware of
the need to keep me. When I went in and said, "I have to
have this to get reelected," they were very responsive. That
was one currency they couldn't negate. . . . Then they asked
me to serve on House Administration.

Although the freshmen frequently found the House leadership
responsive to their wishes, it was apparent to several that policy
viewpoints were taken into consideration when assignments were
being made to some committees.

There was rampant rumor that policy viewpoint was a factor
in the Democratic assignments to the Commerce Committee,
where there was a big fight over the subcommittee chairmanship of the Health Subcommittee. Whether in fact it
was a factor in the Steering Committee's decision-making
process, I don't know, but everybody thought it was.

. . .

When I was being considered for Science and Tech, they
were interested in my views on nuclear power before they
would make any decisions.

. . .

My first choice was Education and Labor, and my second
choice was Armed Services: Education and Labor because in
my six years in the state senate, education was one of my
major bags . . . but Armed Services primarily because of
my background as a Marine Corps Reserve officer and my
interest in national defense.

I was told, initially, Armed Services would be more difficult to get than Education and Labor because it was a more
major committee. But then they found out I was a little bit
of a moderate Republican, and the word came down that I
wouldn't feel very comfortable with John Ashbrook
[Republican, Ohio] as my ranking minority member, that
they were too ultraconservative, and they were afraid I
might vote with labor a couple of times, or I might vote for

the Department of Education bill, so I would be better off if I began to realize the fact that I wasn't getting on Education and Labor, but they were going to save me by putting me on Armed Services.

In effect, I didn't get Education and Labor, because I think I am too much of a moderate. I think I was intentionally excluded by the leadership from being on Education and Labor.

However, I got a committee that was just as good as far as I was concerned. I really like national defense issues. It gave me a chance to deal a little bit with foreign policy because you get into the SALT talks and all that bit.

Although the freshmen felt the constraints of their junior status, the atmosphere of the current House of Representatives permits assertiveness on the part of freshmen. Both Republican and Democratic members of the class of 1978 sought and gained significant committee assignments and rule changes for their class. The efforts of the freshman Democrats were summarized as follows:

Our class was active in promoting that there should be freshmen on Appropriations. . . . We put in a specific request to Ways and Means and Appropriations. . . .

In caucus we voted in a way that would elect people to work with the freshmen. . . . We voted as a bloc to support Jim Shannon's [Democrat, Massachusetts] desire to be on the Ways and Means Committee, and we were able to knock out some more senior members. . . .

We were pleasantly surprised to get three on Appropriations. We also ended up with two freshmen on Budget and with a freshman on Rules, which we really hadn't, as a class, expected any chance of getting.

The Republican freshmen also sought assurances from their leadership.

When the leadership came into the orientation program and they all appeared before the class, we asked for a commitment that they would try to get a freshman on the Appropriations Committee, on Rules, and on Ways and Means.

Some of us were a little bit more adamant. We wanted a commitment that we would be [on those committees]. Some [who] were more reasonable said that the leadership had enough problems and we should let the leadership try to work it all out. And so we basically bought a good-faith understanding that the leadership would do what they could on the major committees, but that every member of the freshman class would get on at least one major committee.

7

GOP freshmen were also involved in a major change in the rules by which the party makes its committee assignments. A freshman participant explained the change.

It has always been done by the executive committee of the Committee on Committees. There has been a revolution in the way Republicans are assigned to committees.

Before, the senior guy from each of the big states—like Bob Wilson—would sit on the committee and cast seventeen votes because there are seventeen Republicans from California, whereas the members from states with only one Republican had only one member, Don Young.

Young, from Alaska, would sit there, and he might represent fifteen single-state members, but he had only one vote, instead of fifteen, and that is the way it had been for sixty-five years. And there were all those one- and two- and three-member state delegations—the people that represent all those states were always appointed by the leader.

But in a conference here a couple of weeks ago, we changed all that, so now it is one man, one vote. The guy from the one-member state will cast fifteen votes if that is how many members he represents, and the minority leader no longer has the power to appoint those people. We will caucus and choose them ourselves.

So, instead of the big states—the top five or six, Ohio, California, and so forth—dominating all the key assignments henceforth, it will be one man, one vote, on the executive committee of the Committee on Committees.

In analyzing why freshmen were able to exercise as much influence as they had in the organizing of the House in 1979, the freshmen discussed the effect of the changed ratio of junior to senior members and of the reforms of the early and mid-1970s.

The seniority system may be very strong obviously, and yet because of the numbers of first and second termers, we have become more of a potent force. . . . I think that the newer members have been more willing to participate in the process, and the senior members have been more receptive to that because people who have been here three terms or less are a majority of the members of this Congress, and that is a significant change from just a decade ago and back through history.

• • •

The biggest change, I think, without having been there four years ago except working for people who were there, is the fact that the leadership is all elected. I just think that that is an extraordinarily important change—electing subcommittee chairmen in real elections, where you have fights, and electing committee chairmen with real elections. . . . They are much more inclined to look upon that new group [of freshmen] as potential constituents in their elections. And when you go to their office to talk with them about your committee assignment, they are looking for ways to try to help you, just the way we look for ways to help our constituents when they come to see us. I think that is a very big factor.

Setting Up Washington and Home District Offices

The transition from candidate to representative requires that each member create in a few short weeks an efficient office organization—both in Washington and back in the home district. Important concerns in setting up an office include maintaining close ties to the home district, maintaining continuity with selected activities of one's predecessor, gaining essential staff professionalism without sacrificing sensitivity to district interests, finding an appropriate division of labor between the home district and Capitol Hill offices, and developing an organization compatible with the leadership style of the new member.

Given the importance of the member's office to political success both in the home district and in Washington, it is not surprising that new members were counseled to proceed slowly in organizing their offices.

A veteran congressman from my state was very helpful in giving me a lot of advice about staffing and operations. And I think that the best advice she gave me was right after the election, which was to go very slowly, don't hire anybody, wait, see what you want to do.

And we were advised of that repeatedly in our orientation sessions—"go slowly; you don't have to rush." And I followed that advice and hired very slowly, and it wasn't until just before we went on the payroll on January 3, that I had completed hiring my staff. And I suspect that was true with a lot of us because we did get this hammered into our heads to move slowly and see what we really wanted in the way of staff.

I hired the best people out of my campaign and then stole people from other places. I had the advantage over some new members, having worked in Washington, and I knew a lot of people around Washington. I hired three people from the Democratic National Committee, that I had worked with. I stole them from the Democratic National Committee.

I stole an LA [legislative assistant] from a foreign policy organization here in town, who was first rate. I did that around town, picked out good people and tried to lure them away. Some, I couldn't get . . . people I had worked with in the past.

. . .

I think I heeded that advice to go slow and ended up with a staff that I am comfortable with. I was able to retain some of my predecessor's key staff people—his administrative assistant, who has worked here for quite a few years, several other key people, and then brought in some others that I had known from [home state], a couple that worked on the campaign.

One of the big changes I made was to keep a few more people in the district than he had done . . . which I think was a proper move to make as a new member. We have, I think, a very harmonious, good working staff. I am pleased at the way it worked out.

The volume of job applications was extraordinary.

. . .

I mean it was absolutely unbelievable, hundreds of resumés. We ended up with about 3,600 resumés.

As these statements indicate, the freshmen were concerned about having a staff with experience and knowledge of the home district. Frequently, this meant hiring individuals from the staff of one's predecessor—even when the predecessor had been of the opposition party.

Well, when I came down, I had no legislative experience. I replaced a member who had been here for thirty-two years, and I hired his aide, figuring that that would allow a transition. . . . I left a lot of the hiring to an aide, and I would interview at the last minute. What I wanted was a totally professional staff down here, people who had experience, because I had absolutely none.

. . .

And so we moved all of our casework to the district. We have a much bigger district staff than my predecessor. We also hired three of his people, including in his hometown. I ran against him twice, but we convinced the woman who had run his district office in his hometown for eighteen and one-half years to come and work with me, which allowed us to then make a real transition in terms of loyalties, institutionally, in that part of the district, and that is the area I tend to lose.

Some new members placed a higher priority on sensitivity to home district concerns than to Washington experience.

In doing a lot of interviewing with the Hill people, I really got turned off by them. I wound up only hiring four Hill people, and I basically hired fourteen hometown people. And the reason for this was that I found the Hill people were very much concerned about being a professional. "But don't tell me about your district." "Really, when I worked for the former congressman, no, I never went back to his district." "Oh, yes, I went back twice a year"—you know, no appreciation by the Hill professional of what the district is like, the problems you have in your district, the need to be sensitive to the problems that are generated by the district.

So, I just said, okay, you know, I will take the disadvantage of inexperience, but have the kind of people who can relate very much to the district I represent. And I wound up actually letting three of the four Washington people go after awhile.

· · ·

One of my problems in the campaign was that I was accused of being a carpetbagger, not having lived in the state for ten years when I ran for Congress. And so I was super-sensitive to [name of state] things, I guess, and I was fortunate enough to pick up, for my experienced Hill personnel, people who had worked for as much as twelve years for the Republican senator, who had just retired and had very competent people. And I hired three of his people to work for me back in the state. I picked up his top press and legislative person to work for me here.

So, I inherited a professional Washington staff that had a lot of background experience, in the state, which was very helpful. I picked up a couple of people who had worked for me previously. My secretary, who has worked with me off and on now over the years, and who came out and campaigned for me for a year, but who knows Washington very, very well, is from Pittsburgh.

But in terms of the breakdown, we do most of the casework in the district, although I have only got about four people out there. The rest of them are here.

In my state, we still are fairly traditional in the way we do things, and none of my predecessors, either in the House or in the Senate, had really done a very sophisticated job of working the district. Nobody had ever thought of a mobile office, and if a mobile office is justified anyplace, it is in a 98,000 square mile congressional district, so we have got a mobile office, and it has gone down very well.

We are doing a more sophisticated job of working the district than anybody else has.

Each freshman representative was running a separate and individualized political enterprise. As a result, the organization of congressional offices ultimately reflected members' preferences, as the following comments indicate.

> I delegate very, very intensively. And I would say that we basically applied the theories of Peter Drucker and one management consultant that we are still using.

> • • •

> I intentionally did not want any kind of a big AA [administrative assistant] from the Washington establishment to run my office. I run the office. You know, I want access to the staff. I want to make the decisions. I interviewed everybody. And I have also fired a few already.

> • • •

> I have a bunch of twenty-five-, twenty-six-, and twenty-seven-year-old people who are all extremely bright and do a good job, but . . . they don't have anyone to direct them. . . . We are running it as a troika.

The Workload

One of the things that shocked the new members was the pace that they were expected to maintain. They were not fully prepared for the sheer busyness of the place and the demanding schedule even though some had worked in the Congress before.

> We are talking about the incredible busyness. Now, another member of this roundtable and I were here before, as Congressional Fellows, and I was aware of how busy Gerald Ford was, and how busy Mark Hatfield [Republican, Oregon] was, but I never thought that I would be that busy as a new member, and have all those different pressures on you.

> • • •

I think the biggest shock that has been coming through, the biggest shock to me, as a new member, was this busyness. You are a piece of meat shoved from one meeting to another. That was the biggest shock to me . . . the insanity of the scheduling and the fact that you go to so many meetings. I don't question the veracity of my colleague, but his vast preparations for his committee meetings and subcommittee meetings—I don't have the time to do that. If I am lucky, I am extraordinarily lucky if I can get an LA to give me a five-minute briefing on who these witnesses are that I am going to hear.

Serving in the House as a Career

During the twentieth century, the House became professionalized, and long careers became the norm. In the 1970s, however, voluntary retirements became more common and membership turnover increased. The freshmen of the class of 1978 were not thinking of lifetime careers in the House as they began service in the chamber.

I don't know. I guess I will stay as long as I am interested and I feel it is a challenge, but I don't feel a long-term commitment and I don't know what comes next. I just decided a year ago that I was going to run for Congress, and my thirteen-year-old keeps asking me what I am going to be when I grow up, so, you know, anything can happen. I don't know what I am going to do.

. . .

It is very much a two-edged kind of thing. I had a predecessor who served ten years, and a lot of us in our area were surprised when he retired after only ten years, because he was regarded as safe and could have it as long as he wanted.

Now, I understand why, after ten years of this crazy life, never seeing your family and whatnot, you would bag it, particularly when you represent a district where you never have a life of your own, and your family really pays a price. So, on the one hand, I think, well, after six or eight years, if I am fortunate enough to be reelected, I can't imagine wanting to do it more than that. On the other hand, I can see the enticements. You might get a subcommittee chairmanship, and then you are able to do more, and then you would have some desire to want to hang on. . . .

If I were here eight years and sick of all the running around and the insanity of the scheduling and the burdens on my family, I might be enticed to stay on because of the increased ability to influence the issues I care about.

It is very much two-edged in my mind right now as I look six, eight years ahead if I can get reelected.

. . .

I would like to be here. I think I would like to try to live a contradiction—I would like to be here as long as I can, and I would like to live each term as though it was the last term, because I think you run into real problems if you start thinking about being here very long. You start automatically short-changing risks and short-changing confrontations, and not doing the tough things you ought to do. And somehow I hope to be able to convince my constituency that it should accept my living those contradictions.

. . .

You know, I have given up politics twice before, and this is the third time around, and I have finally reached the point, I guess, where I admit to myself that I am a junkie, that I like it.

It's the kind of thing where, if I could sit down and spell out what I would like to do with the next year, what I would like to do with the next year is be right where I am, doing what I am doing.

I can't say that I anticipate or that I want to spend the rest of my life doing it. . . . There are costs associated with it. There are other things that would be fun to do, that I am precluded from doing now. There are obligations coming up down the road, kids have got to go to college, and it is very difficult to do on a congressional salary, as I think everybody knows.

So, I try to have a short-timer's attitude, to some extent. I am fortunate to have a relatively safe seat. I suppose I could stay for what I want. I look forward to being here for some period of time, although I don't ever want to get to the point where I think I have found my career pattern. I have never held a job longer than two or three years in my entire life, and I am reluctant to make that kind of a commitment.

3

Working in Committees

Specialization

The aggressiveness that the freshmen demonstrated in seeking their committee assignments carried over into their committee work. After only a few months of service in the House, they found their committee work rewarding, and they were able to participate actively in spite of their junior status. The need to specialize in one's committee work became apparent at once.

> [Committee work] is critical for me. That is what it is all about. It is what I really enjoy. That is why I am here.

> • • •

> Unlike the state senate, committee work is the only area you can contribute to effectively here. You know, in the state senate, where there were only fifty people and you were on five committees, you pretty much knew everything that was going on. When a bill hit the floor, you could have an amendment. . . .
> I find down here—I am only on Armed Services with two subcommittees—and I find out that that is *the* area where you can make your most positive contribution.

> • • •

> The time we spend on Education and Labor, where I am on two subcommittees, on two Education subcommittees, that is extremely significant, and the *one* place probably where you really can have an impact on legislation.

As they discussed the politics of their committees and the individuals who wielded real power in committee and in the House, the freshmen made frequent allusions to the importance of knowledge and expertise, as in the following description of Appropriations Subcommittee chairmen.

15

I guess, from my observation of Appropriations, it is simply knowledge that really matters. You know, I think the fact is that Eddie Boland [Democrat, Massachusetts], who chairs the HUD Subcommittee, knows more than all the rest of us combined, because the rest of us run from subcommittee to subcommittee. We get portions of things. Well, he has been doing it for years. It is just incredible, the background and knowledge he has. Plus the chairmen are there day in and day out. And in Transportation, there is Bob Duncan [Democrat, Oregon], in his first year as chairman, but he has just worked very, very hard. And, you know, clearly, the chairmen of those subcommittees have much, much more impact. The rest of us have impact to the degree we can affect the conclusion of the chairmen.

They write a bill. We don't get a bill in to start, and what we basically deal off, when we write a bill, are the chairman's suggestions, and there are very few changes. But that has to reflect and feel for what the committees are willing to accept.

The freshmen were also impressed with the procedural powers of the chairmen.

In the Education and Labor Committee, where Carl Perkins [Democrat, Kentucky] has been for a long, long time (and he also serves as the chairman of one of the subcommittees on Elementary and Secondary Education), I find his real strength is that he has the proxies. We have had some votes when he has ten, twelve proxies, and he goes through with it. And I think, kind of out of respect as a very senior member, he really isn't challenged.

Lack of an Apprenticeship Period

Even though seniority and expertise are important sources of power in committee, the freshmen did not feel inhibited about challenging senior members in committee and taking an active part in committee decisions. There was also a strong belief that aggressiveness and hard work paid off with influence even for members with low seniority.

There's no apprenticeship period. . . . It goes back to the fact that a lot of us came out of the state legislatures, and we are not in awe of anything down here, and pretty much understood the process.

. . .

I don't think I was awed by, you know, the committee, but I must say that when I first came down here—my background is as a trial lawyer and assistant district attorney—and I went to some of these hearings, for instance in Aviation, and I heard them talking about what they did to engines and everything else, and everybody else knew what they were talking about, I felt my brain had atrophied. I really was concerned. . . . But it dawned on me that they had discussed this stuff for two and four years, and now, you know, I fit right in with the language, too, because I have done a tremendous amount of reading.

. . .

On the Interior Committee, the chairman has a standard rule that whoever gets there first gets to ask questions first. There is no such thing as seniority in terms of the five-minute rule. . . . If I am the first guy there in the morning for the hearing, and the guys on the committee have been there twenty years, they have got to wait until I finish, because I was there first.

. . .

We do that on the Foreign Affairs Committee, too. . . . That is a great rule . . . a very practical rule. The people show up, and we start on time. All the committees ought to have it.

. . .

My experience in committees has been that the members, even the younger members, are perfectly willing to just ride roughshod over the chairman and the ranking member. They don't have any qualms about it at all, and it happens all the time, on amendments, on procedure, on whether or not we should or shouldn't report a bill. It is not at all unusual to see the chairman badly defeated.

. . .

The proxies don't always go to the senior guys either. . . . I, as a freshman, have voted wads of proxies.

. . .

No, they [proxies] go to the person who has the energy and the drive and who does his homework. On House Administration, two people have all the real votes. On the Republican side, is Bill Frenzel [Republican, Minnesota], who was fourth ranking at the beginning of the year, and he clearly is 90 percent of all Republican activity in House Administration. And on the other side, it is Frank Thompson [Democrat, New Jersey]. I mean when Thompson wants to, Thompson totally runs that committee.

I think the key is persistence and guts and toughness, year in and year out, knowledge in the sense of the Eddie Boland kind of knowledge: that eight years ago, I did you a favor, and I need your help on this thing. . . .

Changing Committee Assignments

Initial assignments to committee, of course, are not always satisfying to new members, who may decide to seek new assignments in the next Congress. The freshmen noted that a desire to switch committee assignments caused their colleagues to be especially sensitive to the party leadership's wishes on key roll call votes on the floor.

There's an exception to people putting their constituents ahead of the party leadership. Folks who are worried about changing committee assignments are much more sensitive to how they're perceived by the leadership. . . . It basically reflects the fact that once you are here, if you are situated where you want to be, then you're on your own track. But if you want to change, that makes you more sensitive.

When members do seek to change their assignments, it is necessary for them to go through much the same kind of campaign that they used in gaining their initial committee slot. Two members described their efforts to switch committees after the 1980 elections.

I went and talked to all the Republican members of the committee—William Broomfield, Edward Derwinski, Millicent Fenwick, and on down the list, and to John Rhodes [minority leader] and even some of the Democrats, and evidently my name was one of those that Broomfield suggested. . . . I also went to our guy on the Committee on Committees. . . . Yes, I campaigned for it.

• • •

I stayed on Armed Services and got on Merchant Marine and Fisheries for very parochial reasons. . . . I had to go around and write letters to everybody on the committee. . . . I worked through the dean of our state delegation. He is the senior Republican from my state. He happens to be on the executive committee of the Committee on Committees, and, you know, there's a game they play; they trade off, and he goes in with thirteen votes from my state, and Frank Horton from New York has X number of votes.

The Effect of the Budget Process

During the Ninety-seventh Congress (1981–1982), the House was preoccupied with the budget, as budget resolutions, reconciliation bills, tax legislation, and continuing resolutions dominated the congressional agenda. This resulted in the belief that the traditional role of the authorizing committees as the shapers of public policy was being seriously eroded, and in a feeling of frustration among members not serving on the Budget Committee.

> There is very high level of frustration on the part of the authorizing committees. We spend all our time on the budget . . . that is, in fact, where the action is today. The Interior Committee ends up with fourteen bills on the suspension calendar the week before we're going to adjourn because we haven't been able to do anything else all year. You get these things coming up only under suspension of the rules that are really major items that ought to be debated and ought to be considered. But we simply haven't had the time, so that in the last week of the session they come up and we try to suspend the rules and pass a fundamental change in our ongoing relationship with the Soviet Union over economic sanctions. It's got no business on the suspension calendar.
>
> · · ·
>
> There is a frustration level. For example, I've spent a good portion of the last year working on one bill, as chairman of the subcommittee, and we've busted our rears. We got an authorization bill through our committee. . . . I spent a whole weekend in meetings hammering out the agreement on this, and our authorization bill is clearly not going to come to the floor this year. A portion of it was tacked onto the supplemental [appropriation bill] and went through that way. All our efforts—we worked out these difficult compromises on how the money should be expended—were wrapped up in a two-paragraph letter from the cabinet secretary saying that the administration will, to the extent possible, attempt to use the authorization bill passed by our committee as its guideline for how to spend the money included in the supplemental. That's frustrating . . . we kill ourselves, and the bill will never see the light of day as best as anybody can determine at this point. . . .
>
> But on the other side of it, there's nothing in my work that is anywhere near as challenging and exciting as the

ability to get into issues the way you can in a sub-committee and full committee. . . .

. . .

One of the things I'm going to do is to go for a subcommittee chairmanship on one committee and try to get on the Budget Committee in place of my assignment to another. That's where the action is going to be in the next Congress.

4
The House Floor

To the uninitiated and to the tourist, observing the House in session is frequently a disconcerting experience. Members can be seen milling about, chatting with each other, reading, signing their mail, and seeming to pay scant attention to the debate. This can lead to the impression that what happens on the floor of the chamber is unimportant and purely ritualistic. The freshmen quickly learned, however, that the House floor is important as a communications mechanism. It is on the floor that they have an opportunity to talk with their colleagues.

The Floor as a Communications Network

You put your finger on it when you said communications. That's where I see the other members.

. . .

You sure know better what's going on in the House if you spend a little time on the floor because you just pick things up; you overhear things; you butt into conversations; you're asking your people what's happening in their committees. You're much better informed, and I never call another member on the phone in the office. If I want to talk to somebody, I just look for them on the floor and you can grab them and talk to them.

. . .

As a freshman, I really don't have much contact with the chairman of my committee. But if I have an idea, I will say, "Gee, this is what I'd like to do," and sit down and chat with him while we're waiting to see what happens on a vote and then follow up with a letter. That works, and it's good . . . when something major happens like the ethics investigation and scandal, the place where you're really going to talk about that, where you hear the most about it, is on the floor. Especially if you're not involved in the committee, the floor's just buzzing with that stuff.

Taking Cues

Each session when the bells ring in the Capitol and the House office buildings calling the members to the House floor for a record vote, the members stream into the chamber. Oftentimes the vote is on an amendment, procedural motion, or bill which is of marginal interest either to the member or to his constituents. In such circumstances, a shortcut to reliable information about how to vote intelligently and responsibly is essential. Members reported that they frequently take cues from their colleagues on how to vote.

> If you had a vote coming up on an appropriations thing, and you respected a fellow member, you would go to him and say, "What is the story on this?" And I tend to do that. When I come into [the House chamber], particularly on an amendment, when you have been at a committee meeting or whatever, and you don't have any idea what it is, you tend to look around the floor for somebody you know, who is on the committee, whose judgment you respect, and you go to him, somebody who you expect is going to vote pretty much the way you normally would.
>
> So, in that sense, the expertise and the committee's specialization are very important, I think, to me.
>
> • • •
>
> I think the other members become much more influential than highly paid lobbyists. . . . Who do you listen to? To some lobbyists . . . or do you listen to some other member, like Bill Frenzel, who is a well-respected member from Minnesota?
>
> • • •
>
> And I think this goes across party lines. I have a lot of respect for Paul Simon [Democrat, Illinois]. I served on a subcommittee with him. But I think that the other members are very influential, and we recognize it. And why are they influential? I think because they have exercised good judgment, have expertise in the area, and know what they are talking about.
>
> • • •
>
> Many guys vote based on how one of the other members

of their [state] delegation voted, and not necessarily on the merits of the amendment.

I find that a lot of times, people walk in, and the first thing they do is look at the board, and they have key people they check out, and if those people have voted "aye," they go to the machine and vote "aye" and walk off the floor.

I read all that background stuff—the Democratic Study Group stuff—in the morning before I go to vote—now, I go on the floor, unless it has been something that has been amended and substituted, so I don't know what is going on, I will go in and kind of know where I am going.

But I will look at the board and see how [members of the state delegation] vote, because they are in districts right next to me and they have constituencies just like mine. I will vote the way I am going to vote except that if they are both different, I will go up and say, "Why did you vote that way? Let me know if there is something I am missing."

House Action on Committee Bills:
A Decline in Deference to Committees

There was a feeling among the group of freshmen that committees were having an increasingly difficult time defending their bills on the floor of the House. That is, the committees were being "rolled" on the floor, and deference to committee decisions was being eroded. The freshmen felt little obligation to support committee decisions. Junior Republicans suggested that one of the reasons they often opposed committee recommendations was a tendency for senior Republican members of committees to become too cozy with their influential Democratic colleagues.

I think it is fair to say there is a feeling on our side of the aisle that oftentimes the senior Republicans on a committee have sold out to the Democratic leadership on the committee. . . . If you look at the Department of Education vote, we had an overwhelming vote against the department on our side of the aisle, but Frank Horton [Republican, New York, ranking minority member of the Committee on Government Operations] was leading the charge [for the creation of the department].

There was also a feeling of general skepticism about the work of the committees and their tendency to be special pleaders for the causes that fall under their jurisdiction.

It may be even more fundamental than that. It may go back to the view that some of us have, that the committees are

23

advocates. They largely tend to be advocates for whatever
their subject matter is. I mean you tend to find farmers on
the Agriculture Committee. You tend to find people from
ports on the Merchant Marine Committee. And there are
some who make the argument that if you represent a farming
district, you shouldn't be allowed to be on the Agriculture
Committee, or at least there should be some balance, or
whatever.

And so a lot of us tend to be skeptical, minority or majority. We aren't going to instinctively support committees.

. . .

The argument that I disregard most on the floor, as an
individual member now, is that the committee has reviewed
it and thinks this is the way to go. That is meaningless. . . .

I just don't buy that you are going to do this, or you are
not going to do that, because the committee thinks this is a
better way to go. That just does not affect me at all.

. . .

I sense that on the Appropriations Committee, especially,
that once they have been through the agony of doing the
bill, there is almost a requirement that the Republicans
come out in support of the position on the floor . . . you
will get a guy like Bob Michel [Republican, Illinois], who is
very active on the Appropriations Committee and is the
Republican whip, oftentimes voting with the Democratic
majority on bills that have been through that Appropriations
Committee process. The rest of us don't feel under any
constraints at all—at least I don't—and the junior guys, the
junior members, don't, partly, I suppose, because we are not
consulted when it comes time to construct major deals on
major pieces of legislation.

A Decline of Collegiality

The lack of deference to committee decisions was viewed by some as
evidence of the breakdown of collegiality in the House and of a
weakening of concern for the House as an institution. There has
been an increase in an advocacy style among representatives, instead
of a tendency to follow the late Speaker Sam Rayburn's admonition
that "you have to go along to get along."

What is happening, I think, is that the collegial system is
disintegrating. We are seeing it begin to disintegrate, the
collegial system, where you were elected from back there,
and you came here, and then what really mattered was what

happened within a mile of the Capitol and those relationships. And you went back home and explained whatever it was that happened here.

There really wasn't a great deal of relationship. You were a representative sent up here, and you went back home and said, "Well, I tried, but, you know, the chairman of the committee did something, and I couldn't get anything done." And they said, "Yes, that is the way Washington works." That is breaking down.

Let me suggest to you that the two most effective Republicans in recent years, in terms of coming out of nowhere and achieving something, have been Henry Hyde [Republican, Illinois] and Jack Kemp [Republican, New York]. In very real ways they have achieved power in the House and in the country that very few other Republicans in the House have—I can't think of anybody who has rivaled them in some ways. . . . And they have both done it by being mavericks, by being very stubborn, by getting outside their zones. Kemp is not on Ways and Means, yet he is the dominant tax figure in our party in many ways and really has an impact on the leadership.

And they do it by using the new forms of power, to the point where Henry Hyde—who is aggressively pushing a nasty issue [antiabortion proposals] that nobody wants to vote on—comes within three votes of beating the classic insider Republican for the conference chairmanship.

The other thing I would say is happening is that because of the computerized mail, television, and the airplane, and I guess long-distance telephones, I think we are becoming a national convention. I think that if you measured the percentage of time we spent in the collegiality of the Congress, compared with our predecessors twenty years ago, you would find that we are affected dramatically more by our constituency, and we live in our constituency even when we are here, much more than our predecessors did.

And as a result, we are less collegial. I mean I have much more concern about how the people in the _____ district of [his state] feel about a foreign aid bill, or feel about Rhodesia, than about how my colleagues on the floor feel.

· · ·

There is a reduced concern for what we do as an institution. . . . Very few people on the floor give a damn what the House does as an institution. We all care about issue positions, not about what kind of legislation results.

5

The Congressional Party

The members' relationship with their party was an ambiguous one. They asserted their independence from their party, but at the same time they felt a sense of obligation and peer pressure to support their party's positions. They tried to avoid confrontations with party leaders, yet they were also surprised that they were not subjected to more frequent and intense partisan pressures. The representatives seemed to enjoy their relative independence from their party, but they were also frustrated when the party was not sufficiently active—as in developing alternative programs to that of the administration.

Members' Relationship with Their Party

I don't even think about the leadership in the sense of a threat. I've voted against the leadership's position on some very key issues. It doesn't show up in the percentages, but the Speaker made an impassioned plea; I was seated on the floor when he made a very strong plea and the majority leader made a strong plea for the Chrysler bailout, and I just couldn't buy it on substantive grounds and on the merits. I voted against their position. It's one of a few votes, percentage-wise, that I disagreed with the leadership, but I didn't consider whether or not this was going to cause any problems for me with the leadership. The Speaker obviously felt very strongly about that issue because he made, I thought, a very effective case for his side of the issue.

• • •

I don't worry about what the leadership is going to think. I truly feel that what I'm doing is I'm voting what's right and that makes a difference for me. I think my vote has been with the leadership in a good number of instances. I don't play follow the leader, but I do have the support of

Tip O'Neill. He came to the fund-raiser for me in November. I have just been appointed by Tip as one of the congressional observers on a presidential commission. I don't know if I am being rewarded, but I have a good feeling about what I'm doing, and I don't think it's because the leadership expects it or demands it. I'm doing it because I happen to concur in a lot of instances.

. . .

Well, I've heard the pitch a couple of times on the floor. The Speaker or the majority leader will come over to the recalcitrant member who has voted the wrong way and explain to him, you know, "We know your district; you can do this. You can give us this one. This isn't going to hurt you back home, and we need it. Look, if we can turn around six votes here, we've got this thing and we've got the guys here who think they're ready to go." It's just very straightforward. . . .

A colleague interrupted to say:

I have not been approached like that, but if I were, I would give the vote to the leadership.

. . .

One thing that surprised me—and maybe this is unique to the minority or the Republican party—is how few issues they really take a position on.

. . .

I'm now one of the multitude of assistant whips, and we meet every Thursday morning in the office of Tom Foley [Democratic whip]. We sat down last Thursday morning. What is our response? What is our program? We now have the president's [Reagan's] program before us. What is our program? Then somebody said, "Well, maybe the Democrats on the Budget Committee will come up with something. They're going to be holding hearings; they'll come up with the Democratic program." That's absurd. That's why I participated today in the announcement of a new Democratic think tank to help come up with some new programs and ideas.

The following is a colloquy between two freshman Democrats about what happens on a close vote on which the leadership is active and fellow Democrats vote against the party. It captures much of the members' desire for independence mingled with their guilt about not supporting the leadership.

REPRESENTATIVE A: And I say to them [the leadership] that I didn't like the idea, because I'm here to exercise my judgment.

REPRESENTATIVE B: Let's be fair though. On a close one like the Department of Education, when people are going to go against the leaders and they know at the last minute if it's gone the wrong way, the leaders are going to be roaming the floor looking for people. . . .

REPRESENTATIVE A: And so they run out like I did.

REPRESENTATIVE B: They will duck in the side, vote, and duck out so they are not there to have their arm twisted. You do see that.

REPRESENTATIVE A: Absolutely.

Although prepared to deviate from party positions on bills, the members still stressed that they believed that representatives have an obligation to their party on important governance issues such as fiscal policy. A Democrat, for example, felt that his majority party during the Carter administration had an obligation to pass budgetary legislation, while the minority Republicans did not have such an obligation.

> What fundamentally bothers me are the problems of passing the extension of debt limit and passing budget resolutions. . . . I have no complaint whatsoever when all Republicans vote no. Anybody can find a reason to vote no, from the left, from the right, from the middle; wherever you come from, you can vote no. You can find reasons to justify it. But it bothers me when the Democrats flake off, because I just think these are gut, basic issues, things that have to be done.

A Republican echoed this sense of partisan obligation for keeping government afloat when he asserted that the Democrats were responsible for fiscal policy while their party held the White House and a majority in the House.

> You support your party's budget when you're in the majority; then the party has the responsibility; the country needs the budget. You can't function without raising the debt ceiling, and if you can't get a vote out of that, out of a Democrat for that, you might as well not have them in the party.

Among the freshman Republicans there also appeared to be a strong sense of partisanship and a desire to achieve majority status. This tended to propel them from a politics of accommodation with the Democrats toward a politics of public confrontation with the Democrats so as to develop electoral issues.

> There is, I think, among freshman Republicans a sense of trying to force confrontation as a strategy, as a permanent way for the Republican minority to operate. More confrontation rather than cooperation. . . . Another way to put it from our perspective would be that we receive absolutely none of the benefits for helping you guys [Democrats] pass your bills. We're never going to be committee chairmen as long as we're in the minority. We're never going to move up, we're never going to be subcommittee chairmen, and as long as we don't have that option, we'll confront instead of cooperate.

> • • •

> We have certain issues that we think are important. . . . It's our belief that it's our job to so structure the confrontations that swing Democrats and marginal Democrats will have no choice. They've either got to leave their leadership or get defeated at the polls. That's how we're trying to design every confrontation.

In their second terms, several members indicated that their immersion in congressional politics had made them much stronger partisans. A Democrat commented:

> I remember at our first roundtable meeting a Republican said that if there were an incumbent Democratic member—even if he were a friend—he would still go out and support the Republican opponent because the important thing was to elect a Republican Congress. And I remember disagreeing very strongly . . . but you want to know something? . . . I have become the most partisan person going, and I have been actively campaigning against Republicans for incumbent Democrats, and I will continue to do so. So I have changed. . . . I have even campaigned against an incumbent Republican in another state, which is going the limit.

Party Organizations in the House

Both parties have policy committees, but as the following comments indicate, they do not loom large in determining how members will vote.

> REPUBLICAN: It's a place where we debate issues fairly extensively and very openly. Then we vote. The members of the policy committee vote. Virtually any member is welcome to come to the meeting, but only members of the policy

committee can vote to take a position. And basically what it does is give an opportunity to air views and then to signify where the leadership and the majority of the party are going. But there is no sense of being bound by it at all. I got a letter from Bud Schuster [Republican, Pennsylvania], who's chairman of the policy committee, at the end of the session, saying that I had voted with him forty-six out of forty-six times, but I didn't know it at the time.

. . .

DEMOCRAT: I don't see our Steering and Policy Committee doing anything close to that. The only thing I think they do is make the committee appointments.

The freshmen did not attach much significance to the role of the Republican Conference and the Democratic Caucus.

REPUBLICAN: It doesn't meet very often—the conference itself doesn't. It's generally poorly attended unless there is some very hot issue to debate, and there is never any resolution in the conference. There's no vote of any kind. We never take a position as a conference. We let the Policy Committee do that.

. . .

DEMOCRAT A: We weren't able to get a quorum for the longest time because Ted Weiss [Democrat, New York] introduced a resolution to have the caucus go on the record in support of wage price controls.
DEMOCRAT B: One position the caucus took really firmly in this Congress was in favor of H.R. 1, the public financing bill, and the party went on record by a very heavy vote in the caucus. That was the only policy position I know of. . . .
DEMOCRAT A: One other was opposing decontrol of oil. . . . That was passed overwhelmingly in the caucus, with the bulk of the people voting the opposite way when the real bill came in [on the floor].

Democrats did, however, accord the Speaker, majority leader, and whip organization an important place in developing party positions on issues.

The policy on our side is set through the leadership and whip system. . . . The Speaker, the majority leader, the whip, and all the assistant whips meet and adopt a position on issues, not on everything. But they adopt a position. . . . Then the guy who is working the door [of the House] gives a thumb up or thumb down to let you know what they have decided when you come in to vote.

Members of both parties expressed admiration for Robert Michel (Republican, Illinois), who became the GOP leader in the Ninety-seventh Congress, especially for personal qualities that they believed were necessary for a person in a leadership position. A Republican who actively campaigned for Michel's opponent in the leadership election commented:

> Michel did a very specific thing the day he won [his election as minority leader]. He got up and made a speech in part of which he said that he really saw himself as an orchestra leader and that he had 191 people playing in the orchestra and that he wanted to coordinate the flow of all the talent on his side of the aisle. I walked up to him after that speech and said if you really mean that, I want to sign on and be helpful. I think he really does mean that. He's human like the rest of us. He gets proud, he gets angry, he gets territorial, but, on balance, he has an enormous capacity for allowing very strong personalities to do their thing, and he helps rather than hurts them.

A Democrat made a similar evaluation.

> I have great respect for the guy. . . . I consider him very much an institutional person. But Michel's strength is the quality of his not being afraid of strong personalities. . . .

One member of the group, who had moved into a party leadership post, commented on another quality that a party leader must have.

> When you get into a situation where you run for office among your colleagues, it's intensely competitive and that's satisfying. You have to be competitive, or you wouldn't be here in the first place. That aspect of it is enjoyable.

This member also noted that the party leadership role is a special track in terms of one's House career. He observed that being in a leadership position gave one the opportunity to become involved in a much broader range of issues and activities than is accorded most members.

> It does give you a hunting license. . . . I can see that for a lot of members who've run for leadership jobs and not made it, it is terribly frustrating. It's nice if you can get on that track; it offers brighter prospects down the road than might otherwise be the case if you're not on the track. It's a track some people chose simply not to pursue because they're more interested perhaps in the substance of an issue—Barber

Conable [Republican, New York] would be a fantastic elected leader of the House of Representatives, but he chooses to be the ranking member on Ways and Means and does a hell of a job at it; that's his choice. I can see why some people feel that they peak out after a few years . . . they decide that's as much as they're ever going to have an opportunity to do, and they move on.

Even though the members of the group acknowledged the critical role played by the party leadership and the advantages of being a part of that leadership, they were discontented with the difficulty that the congressional parties have in developing coherent and comprehensive programs. On the eve of the 1982 midterm elections, a Democrat with leadership responsibilities made the following observation.

The strategy is a very clear one, and Tip O'Neill has said all along that the strategy was to win the November elections. I go to whip meetings every Thursday morning, and Tip has been consistent all along about how this was all going to come together in November of 1982 and to have faith, hang in there, we know what we're doing, and the theme of the strategy, and that's all the strategy he has, is that "it's not fair; it's Republican." That message is getting through to folks. In that respect, I would say you have to give Tip some credit for having beat away at social security and some of these other issues. He's beat that drum pretty consistently for two years. . . .

What we've not done well—and this would be my principal criticism, and it goes beyond the day-to-day operation of the institution—is to come up with anything that can give people of the country the sense that we stand for something positive that is an alternative to the Republican party's program. There was this effort last week—the unveiling of the efforts of the task forces that have been working under Gillis Long's [chairman of the Democratic Caucus] leadership—and you saw the reception they received. I think the reception was probably predictable given the thought processes of the Democratic party right now. The party still hasn't decided where it wants to take the country other than that it doesn't want to take the country where President Reagan is trying to take it.

6
Interest Groups

Although the influence of congressional parties is pervasive, the parties must always compete with other interests for the vote of members of Congress. This can be extremely difficult if the competitor is a sophisticated interest group who can assist the member in a bid for reelection. The following is an account of why members pay attention to well-organized interest groups.

I think everybody got the same visitor—he is from [name of interest group].

He has a computer printout, and it shows on the top sheet how his members nationwide feel on four key issues that he wants to talk to me about, public financing of campaigns, and so forth.

The second page is what the aggregates are for my state. The third page is what the aggregates are from my congressional district. And from the fourth page on down, in a big long list, it lists my constituents, name by name, who are members of his organization and how they voted on each of those issues.

And on the back of that is a list of cards, a whole stack of them, where they have written personal messages to me on the back. Now, this is the guy delivering the stuff from my constituents.

They give you the mailing list. I mean it is yours. And then when he is all through, he says, "Now, every year, an election year, we put out a score card on the members, and if you get 70 percent, here is what you get," and, bang, he sets down a nice statue on the desk, and that is what you are going to get if you get 70 percent.

And then he said, "And, oh, by the way, we have a political action committee, and nobody qualifies for support unless they get 70 percent." That is done very nicely, but he got my attention. I pay a whale of a lot more attention to those little green and white cards I get through the mail, because I know he speaks for my constituents—I have got their names and their addresses—than to the [party] leadership.

It is a much more potent force, and everybody has got that kind of organizational capability now. He has got his computer wired to my computer, and, you know, the thing is just going like crazy.

. . . Well, I was intrigued by the whole process, I guess, that the guy really got my attention. Many political action committees are of little consequence. I mean the PACs are a dime a dozen now. But who else can give me a computerized list of my constituents?

Interest group activity is intense on Capitol Hill, but there was general agreement among the freshmen that the most effective lobbying is that done by people back in the district—grass-roots lobbying.

REPRESENTATIVE A: I think the thing that perhaps would be different from the fifties is that the most effective lobbyists are the ones back home. I think hospital cost containment got beat not by anybody here in Washington lobbying heavily. It got beat by people who were on the boards of directors of various community hospitals back home who personally wrote you a letter or called you on the phone or stopped by to see you. I think this is indicative that on certain issues, the administration, any administration, is going to have a tough time if the local constituency is in any way, shape, or form organized because of the congressmen being more constituent oriented than party oriented.

REPRESENTATIVE B: The most intense lobby all year for something, in my case, was for the Chrysler bailout bill, and that was a classic piece of work in terms of mobilizing local support for it. I just got hammered on that one. . . . I think there is a connotation of lobbying that's not necessarily very fair or accurate. When the Chrysler dealer walks in from your home area and says, "If I go down, it involves this number of mechanics, this number of local people, and these jobs"—that has a real impact. That is a whole different way of looking at the bankruptcy, and when he says, "This is what bankruptcy as a word will do to my situation and my community—this is what my banker said to me"—that's a radically different quality of information from a $300,000-a-year lawyer sitting in your office.

REPRESENTATIVE C: Or even the president of Chrysler coming by—I think we're much more impressed by the local guy that's selling Dodge Darts back home than by the president of Chrysler.

REPRESENTATIVE D: Except what has happened is that the Chrysler Corporation, the lobbyists, the guys being paid $300,000 a year realize that it was much more effective to get the guy in the district to come out and lobby you. I think that that's really where it's at.

REPRESENTATIVE B: The point I want to make is that it's very hard to sustain a grass-roots case that's a lie. It would be very, very hard to have gotten that Chrysler dealer activated if he wasn't really scared and felt that—looking at the information that was related to his real life—it wasn't just a question in his mind of being manipulated by a prominent Washington lobbyist hired by the Chrysler Corporation. . . .

When you get a phone call from a Chrysler dealer in [a small town in the district] who says that if you vote no on the Chrysler bailout, you're going to throw out of work 400 handicapped people in Detroit, you know that's not a piece of information that we'd normally have.

The members also talked about the phenomenon of reverse lobbying—that is, the representatives lobbying the interest groups. A Republican described how he tried to activate the lobbyists on a bill that was in their mutual interest.

You work your colleagues if you get a bill you're really interested in in terms of setting up your own whip organization basically. The other thing—the thing I find myself arguing with an interest group—is to get them turned on to go to work some other member. I had a couple people in my office this afternoon. They're involved in something that's key in my committee, and they were of the opinion that a couple of Democratic colleagues on that committee were with them on this issue. I knew the guys had taken a walk on the key vote, and we lost by two votes on that side of the issue. And I told them that and laid out for them the record of what had happened and urged them to go focus on what I thought ought to be the appropriate target. You do get into that occasionally, if you're going to try and straighten them out on something so they'll go to work where they're going to be effective. They can be an ally.

Organized labor has been a traditional and important part of the Democratic electoral coalition, and as a result there was a close relationship between the Democratic freshmen and labor. Even so, Democrats felt relatively free to go against the viewpoint of organized labor.

> I said that labor was important—labor was the only contributor to my campaign prior to my coming down here. . . . But when I said that labor has contributed to me, I don't think that they own me in any way and again I don't vote simply because it's labor. I vote because I really agree with that side of the issue.

There was also a feeling that labor involved itself in so many issues that its influence was reduced because of a lack of focus.

> Labor is involved with so many issues that I don't think . . . there were two issues that they were not concerned about. I don't think we've come up with one—maybe Davis-Bacon is one—that they might turn totally against you on if you did not support them. But I can't see any other.

Even if labor's position was insufficiently strong to control the Democratic freshman congressmen in any way, the legislators said that they felt a special obligation to give labor leaders advance warning on key issues on which they planned to vote contrary to the labor position.

> You know I voted for Chrysler and became convinced it was the right thing to do. But I was undecided for a while. Frankly one of the toughest things—if I would have had to vote no—one of the toughest things I would ever have had to do would have been to call the head of Auto Workers and say, "I'm going to vote no." He has been a supporter for years, and he supported a pile of my friends for years, and he's never asked for anything.
>
> • • •
>
> But that's the thing. He's been with you and supported you. What you do and what I had to do is what you didn't want to do, which is to pick up that phone and make that call before the vote. You feel that obligation if they have been with you and you're going to go against them—to let them know what you're going to do and let them know why before you do it. That's the pressure that's on if they were big supporters and they helped you get there.

One of the tactics of the interest groups has traditionally been to stimulate mail from group members in the member's constituency. Today, when congressmen have their own computer and direct mail capabilities, pressure mail can provide the sophisticated representative with an opportunity to develop a mailing list of the group's members—thereby giving the legislator access to the group. A Republican described how he developed a United Auto Workers (UAW) mailing list.

> I ran with some union support . . . and I try to work and maintain some of those ties. But the UAW is interesting to me and I'd really like to have their help. I've got two automobile plants, one in the district and one on the edge. I can't get to them, partly because of my vote on the bailout of Chrysler and a number of other things. But they recently had 1,700 UAW members in my district send me postcards on oil pricing, which immediately went into a mailing bank, so that I now have targeted virtually all of the UAW members in my district. It's crazy. And I now have their direct mail capabilities. . . .
>
> And in fact, in polls that we took recently, I rank higher with unionized labor than with nonunion labor right now because I write unionized labor every day. I say, "Hi, I just want to let you know I'm up here working for you. . . ."

7
The Presidency

The president and his program are a major influence on congressional politics. Members of the president's party reported that they were reluctant to go against the wishes of their president and that they did take his views into account when making decisions on the floor.

> I still will make my decision based upon what I think is right, but I support the president, and if I can support him, I will. . . . If there are no valid arguments for me not to support him, I will support him. If there is no real strong interest in my constituency . . . or I feel that it's the right thing, I will support him. He's my president, and he's the leader of my party, and I feel the same way about the leadership, but, again, it's not a follow-the-leader type of thing.

Even strong partisans in the opposition find that their actions are influenced by the president and his standing with the public, as is illustrated by the following comments of a Republican concerning President Carter.

> I would argue that it [the president's popularity] doesn't affect what you say about him and his programs. . . . He was riding high at the end of the State of the Union Message, and although I didn't like everything he had to say and said a few critical things about it, I was very careful. I started by saying that I support the president's recommendations here, here, and there, but I didn't like this. It's tone and style and emphasis in public statements more than it is votes. . . .
> When I go to a briefing at the White House, I get angry, and only a sense of respect for the office restrains me from jumping up and saying, "That's garbage. . . ." I've gotten very upset recently at Brzezinski's [the national security adviser] comments that Jimmy Carter has devoted three

years to rebuilding the defense budget after eight years of Republican neglect. That's from the guy who canceled the B-1 and did all those other things. In a partisan sense, that makes me very mad. I don't go to the White House and come away convinced I'm going to support the president. But I'm a Republican, and I'm partisan about it, and I disagree with him. But in terms of his public support, the extent to which the American people seem to be rallying around—his standing in the polls—I'm careful what I say to my people, if he's in good shape politically.

Because of the obligations members feel toward a president of their own party, members of the president's party felt a constant pressure and a lack of freedom. A Democrat said he felt a sense of relief—but not happiness—when his party lost the White House in 1980.

All my friends keep saying to me, "Gee, it must be terrible now to be a Democrat in Congress. It must feel very lonely, and it must be a much more difficult role." It's much easier now to be a Democrat in the House. The burden—to the extent that you felt the burden of the country, and I think that we frequently did feel it when we had to go to the wall on some tough issues—is lifted totally now. It's really going to be relatively easy to explain things back home. Last night, I met with two different groups of constituents out in the district who were upset about two different elements of the Reagan program. It's so much easier for me now, than it was six months ago, to say, "Gee, yes, isn't that terrible, look what they want to do to us."

Like the Democrats during the Carter presidency, the Republicans in the Ninety-seventh Congress felt the constraints on their freedom of action that were imposed by having their party control the presidency, as the following account of the work of the House Republican Policy Committee demonstrates.

If you go back and read the positions of the Policy Committee in the last half of the Carter administration, you'll see that it was basically the propaganda arm of the Republican party. Whatever Jimmy Carter was for, we were against. We'd construct alternatives and zap them out there and create party positions and raise hell with the other side, but we weren't responsible for governing. Now we are. Before we always had a requirement—not formalized in any sense —that we try to avoid taking positions on issues that were going to be embarrassing to colleagues. If we had a major split on an issue like the Chrysler bailout, for example, where we had a lot of Republicans from the Midwest who were for it, we didn't take a position on the bill. We took a pass. Now Ronald Reagan is in the White House . . . and we find ourselves in a position where most of the time the Policy Committee serves to support the president's position.

As compelling as the pressure to support one's president can be, however, there may still be times when even a group like the GOP Policy Committee will decline to endorse an administration position. The Reagan administration's policy of economic sanctions against the Soviet Union in response to Soviet actions in Poland created serious constituency problems for some Republicans, including the Minority Leader Robert Michel.

[In] the current conflict that developed this week over economic sanctions for the Soviet pipeline, with Bob Michel on the one hand and the administration on the other hand—we took a pass to support the leader.

The 1980 elections, which installed a Republican in the White House and a Republican majority in the Senate, created a difficult dilemma for the Republicans in the House, where they were still the minority party. They wanted desperately to become the chamber's ruling party. This goal, however, tended at times to come into conflict with their governance responsibilities to their party's president.

We took control of the government on January 20, 1981, and we are now responsible for governing, and we don't have the option of doing what we did before we got the White House and the Senate. . . . We have to compromise— on occasion you have to cut a deal with Tip O'Neill. . . . Ultimately you have to govern. Not everybody in our party buys that. In a sense you saw that on the tax bill [1982]. There was a major difference between those of us who felt that passing some bill was more important than making a point to the public about tax policy. . . .

. . .

There is a sense of frustration on the part of House Republicans, especially the younger members. We got far enough with the 1980 election when we captured the White House and Senate to be perceived by the country as being in control. . . . But Tip O'Neill is still in the Speaker's chair. That is, at least for me and I think for a lot of other members, terribly aggravating. But we're caught to some extent on the horns of a dilemma, whether we operate on a strategy that is geared specifically toward taking control of the House, or whether we try to help Ronald Reagan try to succeed as president.

When asked to describe the difference between how Presidents Carter and Reagan related to the Congress, one member emphasized Reagan's willingness to become heavily involved with the Congress.

I think Reagan likes his job, and I was never sure Jimmy Carter really did in terms of the give and take with the Congress. The congressional relations operation is pretty good, but I've seen better. [Bill] Timmons, for example, ran a first-rate operation. Of course, he lost his president [Nixon], who had to resign on threat of impeachment. . . . What the Reagan administration does well is to engage its senior people, like the president and Jim Baker [White House chief of staff]. When the going gets tough and when you really need them, you can pull out all the stops and, by God, they're there for meetings or talks or phone calls or whatever you need. It's a full court press, and there isn't any stone left unturned in order to do whatever needs to be done. I wasn't certain that you could ever convey to Carter through Frank Moore [Carter's aide for congressional relations] the idea that the president had a major problem.

8

The Electoral Process

There was a general belief that party organizations had not been a critical factor in the members' election to the House. The party organization even opposed several members for their party's nomination. Still, most felt a need to build a firm relationship with their local parties.

Role of Party Organizations in Gaining Election to the House

Well, you see, I see the party as a dying institution in the city—let me back up. When I run for reelection, I say X plus Y equals victory. X is what the Republican party can give you. There is a Republican vote, whatever it is, okay. And year in and year out, it varies slightly, but it is a base vote. The Y is what you give yourself.

. . .

I was not the organization candidate. . . . In the primary I ran against two district leaders, and they were very political. One was a city councilman. . . . I won with 54 percent.
  I had no organization. I had nothing. So, I did it by means of, you know, hiring people and just going out and doing it for six months. I went from zero to a majority. The party organization just could not produce, and I do not rely upon them to produce for my reelection.

. . .

I'm being very honest with you; that's exactly the attitude of my city chairman. The chairman of the Republican party will tell you point blank he wants state representatives, state senators, because they control state patronage. The only statewide Republican he's really concerned with is not a U.S. senator. He's concerned with the state attorney general, who's going to be elected for the first time . . . because that means jobs—you know, assistant attorney general [jobs] for all the young lawyers looking for work. He could care less about electing congressmen.

. . .

I was not the party's favorite candidate, and my toughest race was the primary, where I had to run against the guy who was an incumbent state treasurer. I had to build my own organization to do it and sort of go around the party. There is no endorsement there. It is just a wide-open primary. But I have spent a great deal of time trying to cultivate the party ever since. It is not hard to do. I spent a lot of hours—letters to precinct committeemen—and always wrote to county chairmen. I never go into a county before I have talked to the chairman and, basically, I raise money for the party and try to make them my own organization.

. . .

You can look around the floor of the House and see a handful—twenty years ago, you saw a lot of them—today, you can see just a handful of hacks that were put there by the party organization, and there are very, very few of them left. It is just mostly people who went out and took the election.

Reelection

Reelection is a constant concern for House members. Indeed, the freshmen believed that the campaign never really ended. The next campaign and the congressional career are intertwined and inseparable.

REPUBLICAN A: You have two careers. One is you have to be a congressman, but the other is you have to be a candidate. Now, I think when you are in Congress, unless you have a very secure seat, I don't think you can ever stop being a candidate.

REPUBLICAN B: But that is part of the attraction, for me anyway. I basically really like campaigning. . . . I am in a situation where I think, as everybody does, the first thing you start to worry about after you win the last one is winning the next one.

And I don't see any great inconsistency between how I conduct myself as a congressman and how I conduct myself as a candidate. I mean it sort of all runs together, and that is what it is all about.

I have to be able to go home every week and tell the folks what I am doing and why I am doing it, and I earn the

43

right to come back here and do whatever it is I want to do. But it is almost impossible for me to separate the two things anyway.

Electoral success is not just the result of effective campaigning. The members believed that it was important to build an image of strength that would discourage competitors from challenging them.

From the day I took office, we worked very hard to solidify support within the party, to raise money early. Last summer I personally called every Democratic elected official in my district—that is, nineteen state legislators, seventeen members of the Democratic Central Committee in my district—and solicited one by one their endorsements. Then we announced that I had been endorsed by every Democratic elected official in my district well before the time when anybody else would be deciding whether or not to challenge me. All that was an effort to solidify the base to make it clear to anybody who might challenge me in the Democratic primary that he or she was going to have to run against the party. They wouldn't be just running against me. Apparently it worked; I didn't have a primary. If I had had to bet two years ago whether or not, if elected, I would then be challenged in the Democratic primary, I would have bet everything I owned that I would have had a strong challenge in my district, but we worked very hard on it, and it worked —we scared people off.

After a discussion of the effect of presidential campaigns, candidate popularity, and party financial health on congressional campaigns, one member suggested that these factors have their greatest influence nine months to a year in advance of the election. It is then that important decisions are made by potential challengers whether or not to run and by contributors whether or not to give financial support.

Maybe the presidential race has an impact not on election day, but nine or twelve months before the election. That's when it comes time for the party—in my case the Democratic party—to go and recruit somebody to run against me. They look at the various candidates that are available. When the candidates sit down and look at 1980 as a potential year to run against an incumbent Republican . . . and they see the problems that Jimmy Carter has experienced, the strong candidates back out and . . . I probably have less opposition today because of the presidential race.

44

The Advantages of Incumbency

The advantages of incumbency were apparent to each member. Several stressed the dividends yielded by an active involvement in constituent casework.

> My constituents are concerned about how much casework is being done, and for the first time they're getting economic development funds in there. . . . I do more of that stuff than anyone, but that's what they're interested in, and I think you find that out with a lot of people. . . . Peter Rodino [Democrat, New Jersey] is truly a member in the old style —a legislator and chairman, but . . . the most important part of his campaign is getting out and doing constituent services, and I think that's where you have to look at incumbency. I think in my district, if I go back to the 600 people whom I've helped and they tell their kids and relatives who all live in the same district—you know, she's helped us— I'm better off. They're not going to look at my votes. I really am convinced of that.

Some members, while taking full advantage of the resources of their offices, actively solicit constituent casework.

> My predecessor . . . essentially did not use the instrumentalities which the reform class of 1974 created for all of us. He never sent out a newsletter, and he did a nominal amount of casework, whereas I have four [district] offices and try to encourage people to get to the office. . . . If you can't, let us send an ambulance for you.

Incumbency also brought with it a greater ability to raise campaign funds. Indeed, members found that contributions came in unsolicited.

> I'm finding that I'm getting contributions, unsolicited contributions, and it's kind of like in appreciation of me, because I had a lot of difficulty raising money the first time around. I'm also getting large contributions, which I never got before.
>
> • • •
>
> You get unsolicited contributions to a greater extent, but . . . the political action committees are being much more careful in the judgments they make about what's a winnable race, less inclined to give just to incumbents, more inclined to give on the basis of performance because they like your voting record. That's my sense, the reading I get from my colleagues and from political contributors.

The greatest value of incumbency is not having access to more campaign funds but the capability of reaching one's constituents as a public officeholder rather than as a political campaigner for office.

It's dramatically easier to run as an incumbent. My opponent made a vicious attack on me in his announcement statement, and I answered it the following day by mailing 220,000 newsletters. . . .

Electoral Success Builds Confidence

Throughout their initial term, the members expressed concern and deference for the views of their constituents. Their constituencies were seldom out of their thoughts. Shortly after their first successful reelection campaigns, however, there was a marked change in members' level of confidence in dealing with their constituents.

I feel more comfortable now, perhaps less need to be fearful of constituents' views, more confident of my own ability when I get before 200 or 300 of them at a community forum to handle any issue that they throw at me and to get the reasonable ones in the room to be nodding when I complete my explanation as to why I voted for this crazy thing, or whatever. So I do feel perhaps more sense of my ability to be persuasive with my constituents, to frame the issues in a way that works out to my advantage.

. . .

I think you have just a little more confidence after you've survived twenty-seven of these town meetings . . . people just come in and shout questions at you. . . . I think you build up a certain confidence so that even if the people disagree, you can end up not being too disagreeable and survive it all politically. Probably when the votes are cast, it really doesn't make much difference if you took a different position from some people anyway . . . not that we shouldn't continue to listen—but it's being willing to go home a little more confident about . . . defending ourselves if need be, that's a comfortable position.

9
The Second Term

The freshmen participating in the roundtable discussions at AEI were each successful in gaining reelection in 1980 and quickly moved, in several cases, into important leadership positions in the House as elected party officials and subcommittee chairmen or ranking minority members. The busy pace of life in the House that had impressed them in their first months as representatives became even more hectic as they became better integrated into the structure of the chamber.

> You all have asked about the most important change that I see between the first term and the second term, and that is that I'm working five times as hard. Now I didn't think I could work harder than I did two years ago, but I now have so much more responsibility and so much more work, and we all have more responsibility. I'm now chairman, which I couldn't possibly have been in my first term, of a special committee. I'm chairman of a caucus. I'm chairman of a subcommittee and assistant whip. Each one of those is an enormous amount of extra work beyond what I was doing three or four months ago. My subcommittee chairmanship is a full-time job in and of itself, more than a full-time job, more than a full-time job right now because of [a foreign policy issue]. That's the big change between the first term and now.

· · ·

> I find myself involved in so many things now that every time there's a task force or campaign or something or other, I'm involved in it—I'm in the middle of it, and I just find that I'm overwhelmed sometimes. It's just more and more and more. It has not gotten easier. I fake it a lot better than I did before, but it has not gotten easier.

During their first term, the members attached great importance to the freshman class organizations in both parties. These class clubs were important agents of socialization, communications networks, and social outlets for the freshmen. One Republican even said that his fellow freshmen were a more important reference group than the party organization.

> I think the most important caucus is the freshman Republican caucus. . . . I don't go to the [Republican] Conference. I don't go to the Policy Committee that much. But if I am aware that there is a freshman class meeting, I'm more inclined to want to try to make that than any other kind of organization on our side of the aisle.

By the beginning of their second terms, however, the members attached much less significance to their class organizations. Some of the Democrats failed to attend the organizational meetings of their class club.

> DEMOCRAT A: I didn't even make it to our election the other day.
> DEMOCRAT B: I didn't either. Did you?
> DEMOCRAT C: I was at a Policy and Steering [Committee] meeting. Where were you?
> DEMOCRAT A: I was meeting with the foreign minister of Israel.
>
> • • •
>
> REPUBLICAN: I think you get more involved with class organizations when you're a freshman, and after that, you kind of blend into the whole bit. . . .
> There's just not that need for the class organization anymore, I think. . . . We still have a kind of ongoing class in a sense. It's still there, but it's not the same kind of spirit.

In spite of their success as a group in gaining a degree of recognition in the House and their involvement in what they considered important activities, the representatives still had the ambiguous feelings they felt as freshmen about serving in the House as a career.

> I think we get ourselves involved in too many things—we see there is some need, and we try to address the need rather than not having anybody address it, especially when it's in the committee you're on. Consequently, you dissipate yourself. . . . I wonder if you're ever in a position where you actually can run what's happening. Sometimes I think that with our family situations, you reach a point in time when you say that it really isn't fair to your family. Your family is back home, and you're running down here.
>
> • • •
>
> A committee chairman—I'd like to be chairman of my committee someday if I can put up with the rest of it that long

—and that's a very big "if." It's a very big "if"—whether your family can put up with it. Our own schedule is the same as all of yours. I used to wonder why my predecessor quit after only ten years. He was enormously popular and could have kept the seat as long as he wanted. Now I wonder how he made it ten years.

By the middle of their second term, the members of the group had detected a shift in their priorities. Constituency relations were still important, but increasingly that work was being handled in a regular manner by each member's office staff. There was more involvement and emphasis upon substantive issues in committee and on the floor.

> I remember Bob Bauman [Republican, Maryland] talking to some of us as freshman members four years ago saying that you have to decide whether you're going to be a floor congressman, a committee congressman, or a constituent congressman. I thought to myself that I was going to try to be a little bit of all three, but I think I've evolved away from that—a lot of the stuff with my constituents I delegate to a good staff. I'm not that active on the floor, but I have become more active in the committees. . . . I'm the ranking member on a subcommittee dealing with some things pertaining to the handicapped, where I think, frankly, we've won some significant battles with the administration. It has been challenging. We have a significant fight tomorrow morning with the secretary of education on some modifications in the education for the handicapped act. I would say that the committees have been in some ways the most challenging . . . maybe you don't get the headlines, but I think it's an avenue where one can—at the risk of sounding too ideal—maybe really accomplish something or be a facilitator for change.

> • • •

> I spend more time on the issues—more on what we're doing in committee and on the floor.

> • • •

> I spend more of my time in committee and on legislative stuff than I did before. . . . There has been a shift in personal time which I think is more productive, and I think my constituents still get the service, and my name still goes on the letters and other mailings.

> • • •

> I spend more time on party politics and national politics than I did two years ago. I'm called upon a lot more to do more

on certain issues than I was two years ago. I'm not doing constituent stuff; my staff has been doing it. They don't need me. They allow me to do my political thing.

Near the close of the Ninety-seventh Congress in the fall of 1982, the members were pleased that the political system of the House gave them such a high degree of freedom in selecting a congressional role that fit their particular personalities, interests, and political needs. There was a sense of individual satisfaction. But they also feared that the House as an institution was not meeting its responsibilities.

> It's a giant smorgasbord. If you measure the job satisfaction in terms of having this fantastic variety of things you can do if you want to, issues you can get involved in, or styles of operation on the floor, in committee, or with constituents, then the opportunities are endless. If, on the other hand, you measure it in terms of the extent to which the process produces the ultimate result you think it ought to produce . . . then it can be terribly frustrating.

. . .

> From a personal standpoint, I am endlessly fascinated by the place, and I can go out and sit on the floor for hours and watch what is going on and who's doing what to whom and who's talking to whom. It never ceases to amaze me. . . . On the other hand, there are days when I go home at night very worried that the dangers are enormous, that our margin of error as a nation is gone—the margin that sustained us through the forties, fifties, and sixties when we had overwhelming military and economic superiority on our side. We lack a national consensus on some of the major issues of the day, and the House under its present leadership, maybe given its current membership, appears absolutely unable to do anything that is significant with respect to those problems. We end up doing dumb things like we did this afternoon—passing a resolution 401 to 1 saying that we're against the massacre of Palestinians. That's nice but. . . .

10

The Other Body:
Perspectives on the Senate

In spite of their doubts about the functioning of the House, most members of the group had a distinct preference for the House over the Senate. Only one indicated an interest in running for the Senate. Indeed, most took a skeptical view of the Senate as an institution and of senators as political leaders and expressed institutional pride in the House.

> The Senate is a zoo. I have no interest in the Senate. I like the scaled anonymity of the House. . . . The Senate is all personality dependent. It's people who shave the face of the next president every morning. That is just ridiculous. I have no interest in being in the Senate. Is there anything senators can do that I can't? I think the only answers are that they get their calls returned by Jim Baker more easily than I can and they can get on network television more easily than I can. That's the maximum that a senator can do that I can't do.

> · · ·

> I've never liked senators. Those folks don't know much, and they're not very competent.

> · · ·

> There is an aura about the Senate that I don't like. I was on a panel recently with three senators. I was the only House member speaking before the group. There is no edge to them. . . .
> They are spread so thin that they can't hold a candle to House members in terms of substance. Their egos are very big. . . . I think there is a certain pompousness there—pomposity—that I find very difficult to accept. . . . In the House, there is a sense that it's a little raucus at times, a

little rowdy, and the floor can be tough, but you really are in the thick of things. The House is the institution closest to the people, and we do have a legitimate claim to having performed the representative function better than our colleagues in the Senate. . . .

Postscript

As befits a truly representative assembly, tenure in the U.S. House of Representatives is not secure. Rather, it is an insecure existence subject to the constant need to maintain one's standing with colleagues in the Chamber and with voters back in the district. In 1982 the electoral risks inherent in congressional careers were intensified because of the depressed state of the economy and redistricting. Members of the AEI roundtable group were not immune from the electoral effects of these forces, and two members of the group were unsuccessful in their bids for a third term. Nonetheless, the members of the AEI roundtable group reflected the best traditions of the House in both electoral triumph and setback. They were committed partisans who served responsibly as members of the president's party and as members of the loyal opposition. Their constituents' needs and concerns were constantly on their minds, but the members also recognized their national obligations. The AEI Congress Project staff wishes to acknowledge the contributions of the seven roundtable members to the process of representative government and to the furthering of our knowledge of Congress.

A Note on the Book

This book was edited by
Claire Theune and Margaret Seawell of the
Publications Staff of the American Enterprise Institute.
The staff also designed the cover and format, with Pat Taylor.
The text was set in Palatino, a typeface designed by Hermann Zapf.
Hendricks-Miller Typographic Company, of Washington, D.C.,
set the type, and Thomson-Shore, Inc., of Dexter, Michigan,
printed and bound the book, using
Warren's Olde Style paper.

Selected AEI Publications

Public Opinion, published bimonthly (one year, $18; two years, $34; single copy, $3.50)

India at the Polls, 1980: A Study of the Parliamentary Elections, Myron Weiner (198 pp., cloth $16.95, paper $8.95)

Both Ends of the Avenue: The Presidency, the Executive Branch, and Congress in the 1980s, Anthony King, ed. (273 pages, cloth $16.95, paper $8.95)

The Federal Loyalty-Security Program: The Need for Reform, Guenter Lewy (90 pp., $4.95)

The United States Senate: A Bicameral Perspective, Richard F. Fenno, Jr. (47 pp., $3.95)

Vital Statistics on Congress, 1982, Norman J. Ornstein, Thomas E. Mann, Michael J. Malbin, and John F. Bibby (241 pp., cloth $16.95, paper $8.95)

President and Congress: Assessing Reagan's First Year, Norman J. Ornstein, ed. (107 pp., $6.95)

How Capitalistic Is the Constitution? Robert A. Goldwin and William A. Schambra, eds. (171 pp., cloth $14.25, paper $6.25)

The Dream of Christian Socialism: An Essay on Its European Origins, Bernard Murchland (74 pp., $4.25)

Canada at the Polls, 1979 and 1980: A Study of the General Elections, Howard R. Penniman, ed. (426 pp., cloth $17.25, paper $9.25)

The Role of the Legislature in Western Democracies, Norman J. Ornstein, ed. (192 pp., cloth $15.25, paper $7.25)

Liberation South, Liberation North, Michael Novak, ed. (99 pp., $4.25)

British, Political Finance, 1830–1980, Michael Pinto-Duschinsky (339 pp., cloth $17.95, paper $10.50)

A Conversation with Michael Novak and Richard Schifter: Human Rights and the United Nations (25 pp., $2.25)

Prices subject to change without notice.